Amazing
AIRPLANES

D0608129

For Jan and Billy—T.M.
For Henry and Horace—A.P.

The Publisher thanks the British Airways Community Learning Center at
Heathrow Airport in London, England, for their kind assistance in the development of this book.

ISBN 0-439-64065-2

Text copyright © 2002 by Tony Mitton. Illustrations copyright ©
2002 by Ant Parker. All rights reserved. Published by Scholastic
Inc., 557 Broadway, New York, NY 10012, by arrangement with
Houghton Mifflin Company. SCHOLASTIC and associated logos
are trademarks and/or registered trademarks of Scholastic Inc.

12 11 10 9 8 7 6 5   8 9/0

Printed in the U.S.A.   23

First Scholastic printing, February 2004

Amazing
AIRPLANES

Tony Mitton and
Ant Parker

SCHOLASTIC INC.
New York Toronto London Auckland Sydney
Mexico City New Delhi Hong Kong Buenos Aires

Whoosh

An airplane is amazing,
for it travels through the sky,

above the clouds for miles and miles,
so very fast and high!

An airport is the place you go
to take a trip by air.

You check in at the terminal to show
you've paid your fare.

The ground crew weigh your luggage
and load it in the hold.

And then you take the walkway to the plane
when you are told.

The flight deck's where the captain
and copilot do their jobs.
They both know how to fly the plane
with all its dials and knobs.

They radio Control Tower to check
the runway's clear.
They can't take off unless it is,
with other planes so near.

By intercom the captain on the flight deck says hello.

You have to put your seat belt on
before the plane can go!

A plane is big and heavy,
yet it climbs up really high.

It zooms along the runway
and soars into the sky.

Its wings hold big jet engines,
which are loud and very strong.
They suck in air and blow it through
to whoosh the plane along.

When the plane moves fast enough,
the air around's so swift
it pushes up beneath the wings
and makes the whole plane lift.

Soon the plane is in the air,
so now you're on your flight.
The cabin crew look after you
and make sure you're all right.

They bring you drinks and magazines
and trays of food to eat.
And sometimes there's a movie
you can watch while in your seat.

When the journey's over,
the captain lands the plane.
Control Tower has to say it's safe
for coming down again.

You sit with seat belt fastened,
there's a bumpy, rumbling sound—
the wheels are making contact,
and the plane is on the ground!

At last the doors are opening.
Then out you come with smiles.

So give a cheer. Hooray—you're here!
You've flown for miles and miles.

Airplane parts

control tower
from here the air traffic controllers direct the planes and tell pilots when to take off and land safely

flight deck
sometimes called the **cockpit** this is where the pilot and copilot sit

wheel
the wheels fold away while the plane is in the air

hold
this is the space where heavy luggage is stored

wing
the wings are hollow to make them as light as possible and a smooth shape so they move through the air easily

jet engine
jet engines blow out air and gas to push the plane forward—the gas is made by burning fuel

terminal
this is the building at the airport where passengers go to catch a plane